Chicago Calumet Heights Club

Calumet Heights Club

Chicago Calumet Heights Club

Calumet Heights Club

ISBN/EAN: 9783743309715

Manufactured in Europe, USA, Canada, Australia, Japa

Cover: Foto ©ninafisch / pixelio.de

Manufactured and distributed by brebook publishing software
(www.brebook.com)

Chicago Calumet Heights Club

Calumet Heights Club

Calumet Heights Club.

What Powder do you use?

For the best results
Use the best Powder.

CLUB HOUSE PORCH – DUCK SEASON.

D.2178

ALL VIEWS IN THIS BOOK ARE FROM PHOTOGRAPHS TAKEN ON THE CLUB
GROUNDS BY MEMBERS OF THE CALUMET HEIGHTS CLUB.

OFFICERS

OF THE

CALUMET HEIGHTS CLUB

..1897..

◆

A. W. HARLAN, President.

WALTER METCALFE,   A. P. HARPER,
Vice-President.   Sec'y-Treasurer.

Directors:

A. W. CARLISLE,   GEO. H. KNOWLES,
E. H. GOLD,
GEO. E. MARSHALL,   PHILIP D. NORCUM.

House Committee:

A. P. HARPER,   A. W. CARLISLE,
GEO. H. KNOWLES.

Membership Committee:

L. J. MARKS,   J. P. FISHER,
C. L. DOUGHERTY.

Shooting Committee:

WALTER METCALFE,   J. S. HOUSTON,   P. D. NORCUM,
GEO. H. KNOWLES,   S. H. GREELLY.

Rifle Committee:

L. L. DAVIS,   R. B. CARSON,
H. B. BLACK.

5

Members of the Club

•

Amberg, J. Ward	1046 Marquette Building
Booth, Sam'l M	34 La Salle Street
Black, A. C	205 La Salle Street
Black, Henry B	Bank of Montreal
Boedker, H. A	New York Life Building
Bird, J. F	Pullman Building
Carlisle, A. W	Rookery Building
Carson, R. B	315 Dearborn Street
Carson, C. W	3672 Cottage Grove Ave
Chamberlain, C. C	4300 Ellis Avenue
Churchill, Chas. E	Monadnock Building
Chanute, Chas. D	413 Huron Street
Cook, M. E	Board of Trade
Davis, L. L	103 State Street
Dougherty, C. L	Traders' Building
Fisher, J. P	313 Royal Ins. Building
Ferguson, H. A	243 Adams Street
Gillespie, John	474 W. Congress Street
Greeley, S. H	Rialto Building
Gold, Egbert H	Rookery Building
Gibson, C. H	Royal Ins. Building
Harlan, A. W	Masonic Temple
Harper, A. P	172 Washington Street
Hodson, F. A	132 Loomis Street
Hobbs, J. O	452 Jackson Boulevard
Houston, J. S	22nd St. and Centre Ave
Hunt, A. O	173 Ashland Avenue
Holmboe, L	Rookery Building
Knowles, Geo. H	4564 Oakenwald Avenue
Lamphere, G. C	221 Fifth Avenue
Lewis, Fred. S	152 So. Water Street
Metcalfe, Walter	169 Jackson Street

4

Marks, L. J . . . .   Traders' Building
Marks, Kossuth · · · · · · · ·   · · · · ·   · · · 177 La Salle Street
Marshall, Geo. E . . . . 103 State Street
Morgan, J. A . . . . 11 So. Water Street
Mumford, W. O . . . .   Rialto Building
McMichael, Jno . . . . Herald Building
Norcum, Philip D . . . . No. 2 Board of Trade
Orr, Frank B . . . .   50 State Street
Paterson, A. C . . . . Journal Building
Pope, Henry P . . .   . 90 Dearborn Street
Sawers, Arthur R . . . . 169 Jackson Street
Schmidt, Walter . . . . So. Chicago
Turtle, R. A . . .   .   36 So. Clark Street
Wilde, W. A · · · · · · · · · · · · · · · State and Madison Streets
Westcott, Cassius D . . . . Marshall Field Building
Whitman, A. T . . . . 45th St. and Center Ave
Young, Sam'l E . . . . 45 Franklin Street

For information etc., address
A. P. Harper, Sec'y
413, 172 Washington St.

Location of Club

• •

THE Calumet Heights Club was founded about nine years ago by a party of gentlemen hunters of Chicago, who were acquainted with the nature of the country and its reputation as a resort for wild game. The location of the station on the railroad and of the club buildings was determined only after careful consideration and a thorough exploration of the surrounding country, and time has amply demonstrated the good judgment and forethought of the founders.

The club buildings, consisting of club house, keeper's house and dining room, members' cottages, ice houses, barns, etc., are located upon the south shore of Lake Michigan, on wooded knolls facing the lake, about one hundred yards distant from the water's edge. The property is located in Lake County, Indiana, about twenty-eight miles from Chicago, and midway between that city and Michigan City, Indiana.

The club station, known as Grand Calumet Heights, is on the Baltimore & Ohio Railroad, less than three-quarters of a mile south from the club buildings. This close proximity admits of reaching the grounds by a short drive in the club wagon or by a pleasant ten minutes' walk through the woods. A short distance east of the station, on the bank of the Grand Calumet, is the home of the club's game-keeper, who has charge of the club kennels and of the hunting boats, etc., of the members.

TRANSPORTATION.

Very liberal arrangements with the Baltimore & Ohio Railroad render this club the most accessible of any in the vicinity

IN THE WILDS.

of Chicago. Morning and evening trains at convenient hours convey members to and from the club. For residents of the south side, connections with the Baltimore & Ohio trains at South Chicago can be made by means of the Illinois Central suburban trains, or the South Chicago electric lines. The B. & O. fare for the round trip is but one dollar.

In addition, the Lake Shore road touches both Pine and Miller's stations, each distant but four miles from the club house.

CHARACTER OF GROUNDS.

The country about the club is certainly unique. Beginning at Whitings, Indiana, just east of the Illinois State line, a wooded strip stretches eastward, following the curve of the lake shore to Michigan City, a distance of thirty-five miles. This strip is from three to five miles in width, and from the sandy nature of the soil is entirely unfit for tillage.

Ages ago it was doubtless a part of the bed of the lake, but in the lapse of time it has taken the form of sand dunes, now for the most part covered with a growth of pine, oak and other trees and shrubs. These dunes vary greatly, some being in the form of gently undulating wooded hills and dells, carpeted with turf and flowers ; then an almost level space with pine groves of considerable extent, and again, some miles to the east of the club house the hills are of great height and teem with a vigorous undergrowth which renders them almost impassable. Here also are enormous sand bluffs, rugged and precipitous, and partially wooded, forming a view seemingly fitter for some western mountain range than for the threshold of a great metropolis.

In this wilderness, except for a stray hunter now and then, a human being is seldom met with. Exploring parties from the club have usually found a few hours of struggling through the dense underbrush and over precipitous bluffs sufficient to curb their enthusiasm.

Scarcely half a mile south from the club house, between the hills, wanders the crooked Calumet, bordered by a fine duck marsh, and a little beyond that is a series of long sloughs much frequented by mallards and other water-fowl.

GAME.

This entire region at one time fairly teemed with game, but the settlement of the surrounding country has naturally resulted in thinning it out of late years. The deer have entirely disappeared, though there are still an abundance of foxes and coons, and a fair supply of rabbits, squirrels, etc. A wildcat, too, has been seen on the club grounds within three years.

Nowhere in the famous Calumet region were wild fowl more plentiful than in the river and marshes adjacent to the club house. Of late years their supply of natural food has diminished, and it has been found necessary to seed the marshes, and the result has proven very satisfactory. Excellent shooting, considering the proximity to a great city, has been had for the past two seasons. Last spring twenty mallards was high score for one gun, while thirty-eight rewarded two others for their day in the marsh. Last fall fifty-eight ducks was high score for two guns. In addition to ducks, wild geese, swan, jack-snipe, plover and woodcock are found in their seasons; and in the woods partridge and quail furnish good sport for the hunters.

TRAP SHOOTING.

The club has fine facilities for this sport, the trap stands being conveniently situated on the beach in front of the club house, with the lake as a background for the targets. During the close season there is a lively competition at the traps at both targets and live birds. Regular weekly shoots for the club medals are held, for which there is a warm rivalry, and the club boasts many excellent shots among its members.

RIFLE SHOOTING.

An excellent range, with the shooting stands a few rods east of the club house, furnishes a fine opportunity for those who wish to compete for the 100 and 200 yards rifle medals. To the former contests ladies are admitted, and many fine scores attest their proficiency, as well as the interest taken by the fair sex in this form of sport. On Thanksgiving day a turkey shoot is added to the competitive events. Both the trap and target shooting are in the hands of competent committees, who arrange all details of the regular and special events.

FISHING.

The Grand Calumet abounds in bass and pickerel, and many good catches reward the patient angler. In the club house is a mounted pickerel weighing seventeen pounds, taken from this stream. A supply of small-mouthed black bass furnished by the U. S. Fish Commission, was planted a few seasons since, and are now of fine size for the angler, as the supply of food in the river is very abundant and ensures a rapid and vigorous growth. In Lake Michigan, too, a few hundred yards from shore, fine strings of large lake perch are often taken.

11

OUTING.

It must not be supposed that shooting and fishing engross the exclusive attention of the club members, for possibly no other club of like character offers so much in the way of other outdoor sports and relaxations. It is, in fact, as much of an outing as a shooting club, and the largest attendance of the year is in the close season when hunting is prohibited.

It is at this time the cottage life of the club is so pleasant. Parties are made up for visits of varying lengths and all sorts of out-door recreations are indulged in as well as the enjoyment of the perfect repose afforded by the environment.

The club surroundings are of a nature to banish from the mind of the city dweller all thoughts of business cares and worries.

From the club house stretches far away to the north the changeful surface of the great lake, with its firm, even beach of yellow sand, reminding one of the sea-shore. To the south, east and west is the forest, with its many pursuits and fascinations. Each season brings its own pleasures, both to the seeker of relief from the hurry and worry of the great city, and to the lover of nature. No part of the year is more delightful than the spring at Calumet Heights. Then nature is most charming—awakening from winter's bonds. The exquisite coloring of twig and shoot and budding leaf, the songs of myriad birds, busy in their love-making and nest-building, the warm and fragrant breath of the south wind, the first tiny flowers, and later, the blossoming shrubs and bushes, all under the soft, fleecy skies with their spaces of azure blue, appeal to every beholder. Nowhere is there a greater variety of wild flowers than about this region from the earliest delicate wind-flower of spring to the blind and fringed gentians of late fall. Lotus, and lily, and fern—columbine, violet and iris—wild orchids, from the tiny fairybell to the rare moccasin flower ; wild honeysuckle and golden rod these, and scores of others, are here for those who seek them. In May the dells are purpled with countless blooms of the lupine and the air heavy with the scent of blossoming grape. In June the fragrance of the wild rose fills the woods. The song and gay plumage of birds without number add to the scene, and a day or two at this season stolen from the brick and mortar and dust of the city seems like taking on a new lease of life.

As the season advances into summer, the lake shore with its merry bathing parties, is much in evidence. The water deepens so gradually that it is perfectly safe for children to wade or bathe, and the beach with its clean, pure sand, is their favorite playground. Nothing more invigorating can be imagined than an early plunge in the surf, before breakfast, on a summer morning, though the general bathing takes place later in the day. It is amusing to note the unanimity with which the men, in summer, make for the lake immediately on their arrival at the club Saturday afternoons. Just time enough elapses to slip into bathing suits, and they are splashing off the heat and dust of the city like a lot of happy school-boys. The lake is naturally one of the chief attractions of the Calumet Heights Club, with its pleasures of bathing, sailing, rowing, canoeing and fishing, not to mention its fine beach, as firm and smooth as a boulevard, affording an excellent bicycling track from Whitings to Michigan City, a stretch of thirty-five miles.

From the club house and cottages can be noted every change upon the surface of the great lake, reaching away three hundred miles to the north, from the quiet of a mill-pond to the fury of a gale with its thunderous surf-beat on the shore. The effect of the sky colorings reflected on the face of the waters in storm and calm is a series of studies for a painter. Squalls, thundergusts, and windstorms, can be plainly seen as they gather on the horizon, and their course noted and followed. Some of these summer squalls are grand in their short-lived rage and fury, and, not infrequently occur late in the day and are followed by a glorious sunset which appears more beautiful in contrast to the former turbulence. It is noteworthy, too, that in summer when the sun is so far to the north, both its rising and its setting throw their gleams over the surface of the lake as viewed from this favored spot.

Not less alluring than the spring and summer pleasures are those of the autumn, with its pure, crisp air, which invites long tramps and explorations through the woods, or boating trips upon the river, where the glowing tints of marsh and forest form a brilliant contrast to

15

ON THE BEACH — WINTER.

the deep green background of the pines, and the clear blue of the autumn skies.

In the fall of the year, too, in addition to the hunting in marsh and woods, the flyway shooting is much enjoyed. In the daytime the ducks rest in large numbers in the great lake, to return at dusk to their inland feeding-marshes. Strangely enough, their flight is usually over certain well-known courses, termed "flyways." About these points the hunters conceal themselves shortly before dark, and fusilade at the dimly seen flocks, drifting swiftly by over their heads, in the gathering dusk.

In winter, naturally, the scene is greatly changed. The woods are carpeted with spotless snow, and the limbs of the pines, bending under their weight of white, present a most beautiful appearance. The drift ice in the lake is heaped up on the shores by the prevalent north winds, and there freezes solidly in the form of great hills or ice hummocks, often extending into the lake a quarter of a mile or more, and forming, as they glisten in the winter sunshine, a rare scene of polar beauty.

On a mild winter day hummock shooting at the water's edge affords excellent sport, the game being mergansers and other species of northern ducks that pass the winter in these latitudes. In winter too, the pursuit of the fox is popular, as well as rabbit and coon hunting. Excellent skating is to be had on the river for those who are fond of this sport, while a toboggan party on Toboggan Hill, with its steep descent of nearly an eighth of a mile, is something to be long remembered.

The following letter written by a young lady, a guest at one of the cottages last June, will serve to give an idea of

A DAY AT CALUMET HEIGHTS.

" We left Chicago on the 3:30 B. & O. limited, Saturday afternoon, and arrived at the club station shortly before five o'clock, in company with a score or more of other members and guests. A few of the matrons and elders chose the club wagon in waiting, but the majority preferred the half-mile walk through the woods to the club house. It had rained nearly two days in the city and the change from the indescribable mud in the streets, and the murky, smoke-laden air, to the pure, sweet smells of the forest, with its dry, sandy footing, was as refreshing as it was unexpected. My hostess had spoken enthusiastically of the relief and change from every day life she and her friends experienced in these wilds, and I now began to realize it as I beheld the beautiful foliage and breathed in the odors of the wild flowers, and especially of the wild roses which abounded everywhere.

"With the departure of the train the last tie which bound one to the conventional civilization seemed to be cast off. Laughter and shouts and jests were the rule, and it seemed impossible to drink in enough of the fragrant breath of the woods and flowers.

"Coming in sight of the club buildings, I saw an extended row of cottages stretching away on either hand of the central building, all perched on sandy, wooded hillocks, and facing the blue waters of the great inland sea which lay sparkling in the sunlight. A sigh of delight escaped me, for here again was the sea-shore of my childhood, with its broad beach of sand and nothing but sea and sky to the far horizon. To the east and west, only the curving shores with their background of pine-clad sand dunes.

"After a change to comfortable outing attire, supplied by my hostess, we sauntered west on the beach, a few hundred yards, to the 'wreck'—a large three-masted schooner, blown ashore in the dreadful gale of 1894, and now standing as erect as if at anchor, fifty yards inland, with masts and boom intact, and imbedded in six feet of sand. So great was the fury of the gale that she was washed bodily over the shallow bars, and where she now stands the water at that time was six feet in depth. Happily no lives were lost, as the sailors all clung to the ship and were able to wade ashore shortly after she struck. After clambering aboard and inspecting the vessel, which included a peep into the narrow dingy forecastle, in which wretched hole I am told the sailors were lodged, we retraced our steps along the beach to our cot-

18

tage, in time for the arrivals by the second train which leaves the city at 4:50 and reaches the club station at six o'clock. Hearty greetings were exchanged on all hands, for the club of fifty members seems like a great family, and I could not help noting the holiday, out-of-school feeling pervading everyone.

"Though so near the city, there is here absolutely nothing to remind one of its existence. The change is complete. I am told the nearest settlement, in any direction, is four miles distant. The only link with civilization is the railroad telegraph operator, whose shanty is one mile away, and with whom the club is connected by a convenient telephone. By this means telegrams may be sent and received, and the operator apprises the club manager of any trains that may be behind time, thereby saving members any vexatious wait at the station.

"The second train had scarcely arrived when the bell for supper sounded, and we were soon seated in the dining room, where the tables were neatly set and the food both ample and substantial. I felt it necessary to apologize for my appetite which, from being very languid at home, seemed to have picked up here to an alarming extent, but my entertainers only smiled and assured me that the Calumet Heights appetite was proverbial and that dyspeptics and others who never know, in the city, what it is to sit down to table with any longing for food, are, after a short time at the club, eager for their meals and can indulge in almost any kind of food in almost any quantity. This is doubtless due to the fact that the members live in the open air as much as possible, and this, with active exercise and relief from the cares of the city, must have a favorable effect on the digestive organs.

"After supper I was invited on the lake to view a most exquisite sunset from a dainty canoe, and, reclining most comfortably on cushions, while my companion plied the noiseless paddle, I think I never realized more keenly the poetry of canoeing. The little wavelets musically lapping the sides of the canoe, the graceful, gliding motion of the fairy craft, the entrancing colorings of the sunset and the afterglow, succeeded by the quiet of

19

INLET.

the glistening stars in the great dome above us, while from the
shore drifted faintly the sound of music and laughing voices, all
left upon my memory an impression not soon to be effaced. The
world seemed far away—a feeling of infinite repose took possession of me and it was with a long drawn sigh of regret that I felt
our keel touch the beach.

" A visit to the club house soon brought a change of mood. In

20

the gunroom the sportsmen were busy with their guns and accoutrements, arranging for tomorrow's contest, exchanging stories, theories and experiences, after the manner of their kind; the club room held a jolly cinch party, with here and there a member with a book; the ladies' room was filled with the life and gaiety of the younger element, while piano, banjo and mandolin were

A CORNER IN THE CLUB ROOM.

spiritedly lending their best aid to song and jest and skylarking. A remarkable transformation had taken place in every one. The trim, citified costumes had disappeared with citified manners, and in place of these were comfort and jollity. Short skirts, leggins, sweaters, blouses, shooting-jackets and hats were indulged in by the ladies, and, as for the men, I was utterly lost. I had occasionally seen dandified specimens of the tourist sportsman, spick and span in faultless regulation attire, and had formed my ideas on these models, but here I beheld the genuine article, and such an aggregation of wrinkled, faded, stained and shapeless garments of corduroy, velveteen, moleskin, canvas and chamois bewildered me. The gentlemen whom I had met on the train in modish attire, spotless linen and dressy head-gear were unrecognizable. Now, I felt, I needed re-introductions all around. 'Yes,' said one, commenting on my expressed wonder, 'We come down here for comfort and change. We can get all the dress and all

21

A COTTAGE GROUP.

the style we want in the city. Here we can wear our old clothes, and there is nothing, I can assure you, so dear to the heart of the hunter as his old shooting suit, with a memory in every smear and stain. 'No,' he laughed, 'those who are seeking for style and functions and high teas must look elsewhere; that sort of thing is tabooed at Calumet Heights.' At this moment he was called to make one of a card game, and sauntering into the club room, he filled and lighted a corn-cob pipe and sat down at the table, a picture of perfect content.

"Out on the broad club porch were groups chatting, and drinking in the beauty of the starlit night, while on the beach, slowly pacing up and down, the forms of a couple were outlined against the horizon—the old, old story!

"Reclining in hammocks, or comfortably ensconced in rockers and easy chairs, I found the family of my hosts on their porch, with some of the neighboring cottagers, and long we lingered in the quiet night, while soft breezes fanned us, and the sound of the waves rippling on the beach was mingled with the distant call of the whippoorwill. My last recollection of this reposeful night was the silver crescent of the new moon high above the trees to the west, and to my mind came, dreamily, Lowell's beautiful lines:

'My day began not till the twilight fell.
And, lo, in ether from heaven's sweetest well,
The New Moon swam, divinely isolate.
In maiden silence.'

"The next morning I, who, at home, idly nibble a little toast at my morning meal, found myself heartily relishing a generous meat breakfast. The wind, during the night, had changed into the north-west, and the air was invigoratingly fresh and clear, while the 'white horses were tossing their manes' upon the deep blue of the lake. I had been invited to take a sail, but the skipper, after casting his weather eye to windward, reported that we would have rather a wet time of it, as the breeze was freshening rapidly, so a party was made up for a stroll in the woods, and I wish I could describe to you, at length, our delightful experiences. Our first destination was riverward to the Second Bend, a mile distant from the club house, and reached by a charming path through the woods. Flowers—everywhere—sprung from the sandy, porous soil, and I am told that no amount of rain or moisture leaves any trace on the surface, so quickly is it absorbed. This, naturally, is a condition fatal to any kind of malaria, and with the piney odors of the woods and the vast stretch of the lake with its ozonizing processes, I should think Calumet Heights would be a remarkable locality for a sanitarium. Indeed, I am told by many of the members that they often run down for a day or two when troubled with severe colds, and never fail to get relief from the change.

AFTER A BLOW.

"We reached our destination, after stopping at First Bend, a bluffy curve of overhanging pines on the river bank, and passing through some charming dells, beflowered with a wealth of wild roses. After resting awhile on a grassy bank at Second Bend, we climbed a tall bluff a little further on and had a fine view of the wild country to the south as far as the eye could reach, the crooked, marsh-bordered river winding to the east and west, while to the north, over the tree tops, we caught glimpses of the intense blue of the great lake. It seemed to give one an extraordinary sense of freedom to stand upon this summit in the midst of such a wilderness. Here one had elbow-room, as it were, for it appeared, indeed, to be the forest primeval.

24

"Homeward bound, we took a path directly through the woods to the lake shore, stopping on the way to repose in a most delightful pine grove whose aromatic odors we sniffed most gratefully. I thought how delightful it would be to pass a morning in these fragrant aisles, with a favorite novel, swinging in a hammock, or perhaps, reclining upon the soft carpet of pine needles. A little later we found ourselves on the broad beach, laden with flowers, ferns and other remembrances of the woods.

"Wind and sea had risen materially, and the waves had a brisk motion which gave us many a scamper to keep from wet feet, as we took our half-mile stroll back to the club house.

"At the club, the weekly rifle and trap-shooting contests were going on. At the rifle range, I watched the ladies do some excellent work with their squirrel rifles at 100 yards, while the men shot off-hand with their heavier weapons, at 200 yards. A telescope fixed on the targets shows the result of each shot, and there was a keen competition for the weekly possession of the medal trophies with their little diamond bulls-eyes.

"The trap-shooting at targets, or clay pigeons as they are called, interested me greatly. I had never seen this kind of sport, and it seemed incredible that the shooters could so often hit the flying disks as they were sharply sprung from the traps. The men shoot in squads of five, from a platform. The trap is sprung from behind as they call 'pull,' and the firing is almost continuous. The spectators view the sport from a shelter in the rear, and applause for skilful work, and chaff for the unlucky, is not wanting. A regular medal shoot takes place weekly, followed by all sorts of matches between individuals and teams.

"Arrived at our cottage, I was aware of a peculiar sensation, one that I had not experienced for a long time. It was yet a half hour to dinner and I, who in the city indulge at noon in only the lightest of luncheons, was in spite of my unusual breakfast, desperately hungry, and the half hour seemed intolerably long. However, the bell rang at last and a merry rush was made to be first served—all except the trap shooters. 'Oh, they can't spare

BOAT LANDING — RIVER.

time for meals,' I was told, 'they have to be driven in.' It was a most substantial meal for me, and I had a little feeling that I was making an exhibition of myself by eating so heartily, until I noticed that the other ladies at our table were no less busy with the viands. I was warned to 'leave room for pie,' as Mrs. Starr, the steward's wife, was famous for this delicacy, and I assure you her fame is well deserved, for anything of the kind more delicious I have yet to eat. For the winter, the lady's buckwheat cakes have a like reputation. 'Pie and Buckwheat Cakes are the Calumet Heights heavenly twins,' said a facetious neighbor, 'We come miles for 'em, literally.'

"My promised sail, which the boisterous lake had prevented, eventuated, in the afternoon, in an invitation to a trip on the river in a duck boat.

"Our start was made from the boat house on the river bank which is in care of the club game-keeper, who resides adjacent to it by the side of the dog kennels. Amidst howling entreaties from a dozen hunting dogs, we embarked in a shallow, tippy craft which swayed with every movement. After I had been deposited on the clean, coarse marsh-grass which filled the boat, with instructions to sit perfectly still, what was my horror to perceive my companion pick up an enormously long paddle and push out into the deep water, standing erect in the tiny, quivering shell. Visions of the damp remains of a velveteen clad young woman being fished out of the weeds crossed my mind, but before I could realize it, we had crossed the deep channel and were gliding through the rushes in shallower water.

"It was a perfect June day, and the pines and foliage and flowers on the bank were reflected in the mirror-like surface with a most charming effect.

"On we pushed, with a steady, gliding motion, through rushes, wild rice, marsh-grass or lily-pads; my gondolier pausing now and then to call my attention to the wonderful marine growth beneath the surface of the river, or to some curious marsh-flower or plant or insect; to the varying shades of green in the waving

ON THE RIVER — SUMMER.

marsh-grass; the formation or coloring of cloud and sky, or, perhaps, to an eagle or a hawk hovering afar off in the blue. He also contrasted the summer appearance of the marsh with its autumn aspect, with its mellow, hazy, sunlight, and the grasses aflame with color, from the palest gold to the ruddiest of browns and russets.

"Nothing seemed to escape his vision, and remarking on this, I was told that all hunters acquire this faculty instinctively—it is part of their craft, and, moreover, that nearly all hunters are Nature-lovers. They see her under every possible condition and in every mood, and no one can possibly be often afield, from the first glow of dawn until dusk, without feeling the companionship of Nature. He had noticed it in the rudest and most uncouth of men, who could find no sort of expression for the feeling.

"Thus we progressed, until we reached a bed of glorious water lillies, which I plucked with bared arms from deep below the surface, my boatman, in the meantime, directing the boat to the finest blooms, and steadying it with the long paddle thrust deep into the mud. In a short time I had gathered a basketful of the beauties. Our trip was resumed with the remark from my companion that he had in view a treat for me, but could not say definitely until he had prospected a little, and, sending the boat along with strong, steady stroke, in ten minutes we landed at a beautiful cove, from which I was led a few yards inland to a sunny slope, and, to my great delight, a bed of luscious wild strawberries lay before me. My guide's fears that they had not yet ripened proved groundless for they were in the very perfection of their delicious flavor. We leisurely ate what we wished and plucked a quart or more to carry home, and then, after briefly enjoying a pleasant bit of scenery from a higher point on the bank, we embarked again, homeward bound.

"As we passed them, the different duck-shooters' 'blinds' on the river were pointed out to me, and in answer to my many questions, I was amazed to find that duck shooting, which I supposed to be a very simple affair, was a matter of so much alertness, skill, experience and knowledge of the habits of the wary fowl that I wondered that any were ever shot—of course this applies to wing-shooting, the art of the true sportsman, and my informant spoke very slightingly of what he termed 'pot hunters'—or those who shoot at birds sitting on the water. Amusing instances were related, too, of the mishaps of novices and of the unpleasant and ofttimes dangerous duckings and mud baths they are exposed to from their ignorance of the art of shooting from a duck boat, or

HAPPY HOURS.

of the use of the push paddle. I was delighted, too, to learn that the songsters and insectivorous birds are never molested by sportsmen, on the contrary they are very strenuous for their protection. This case does not, however, extend to what they term 'robber' birds, such as hawks, kites, jays, crows and the like, who are active in despoiling the nests of the song birds.

"My companion also enlarged upon the physical benefit he and others had derived from weekly outings at the club. He said that to almost every business man there comes a time when the prolonged strain of affairs tells upon the nerves, and especially is this true in times of commercial stringency. Professional men, too, after intense and unusual mental effort, experience the need of rest and change. They all feel if they could only run away from their desks and escape, if but for a day or two, from all that reminds them of their daily affairs, it would be like the lifting of a great burden from their shoulders. The main difficulties usually are, that such relief spots are far away and time cannot be spared for an extended trip. For such, he said, the Calumet Heights Club, within an hour from Chicago and open throughout the year, offered ideal opportunities. One's belongings being kept at the club, there is no packing or preparation necessary beyond stepping aboard the train, and in an hour you are in seclusion and free to follow your bent.

"Thus chatting, we pushed along the crooked stream to the boat landing, and thence homeward, laden with our flowers and berries, and I may say the latter were much relished at our supper table. It had been arranged that we were to return to the city after supper, though I would gladly have remained another night in the happy freedom of this pleasant spot. It was with many regrets that I laid off my comfortable outing garments and donned the starched and stiff attire of the city. For a time I felt as if in a strait-jacket. Everything had suddenly become too tight, and I wondered, impatiently, if our sex would ever have the courage to cut loose from the tyranny of fashion and dare to be comfortable.

31

"Perhaps a score or more boarded the train cityward that evening, nearly all carrying huge bunches of the spoils of the forest, and our car looked like a veritable bower of wild flowers. One young girl carried a basket of the rare lady-slippers, or moccasin flowers, a kind of wild orchid. The blooms were most exquisite, with their tints of white, cream, rose and lavender. The possessor told me she had tramped, with her father, a matter of eight or ten miles that day, and her bright eyes and sun-tanned cheeks were evidence of her enjoyment of her outing.

"With our arrival at the city, ended this most delightful day, and it was with no small pleasure that I accepted from my kind hostess an invitation for another visit later in the season.

"As I recall my many pleasant memories of the day I feel that if I might choose an appropiate inscription for the club portals it might well be:

'Leave *care* behind, all ye who enter here.' "

C. H. Morgan Co.
PRINTERS and BINDERS
11 So. Water Street,
CHICAGO.

ESTABLISHED 1880.

We have a large, thoroughly modern plant and are well equipped for all kinds of commercial work, and shall be pleased to quote prices on catalogues, pamphlets, etc. We solicit your account.

SHOOTING SPECTACLES

FOR

Trap and Field Shooting

If you wear glasses and shoot, you cannot afford to be without a pair of spectacles made for that purpose. Our spectacles are superior in style, workmanship and fit.

Send for Descriptive Circular.

ALMER COE, OPTICIAN,

65 STATE STREET,

Central Music Hall,   CHICAGO.

A Diamond

...as a Bank.

1st.   It pays good interest in the pleasure its beauty gives you.
2nd.   It is everlasting.   It never wears out.
3rd.   It is the best collateral in the world.
4th.   You can borrow money on it instantly.
5th.   It doesn't change in value.
You can invest your money in one the same as you would in a savings bank.   So much a day, week or month.

We carry one of the best assorted stocks in the city.   It will cost you nothing to look.   It will cost you less than you think to buy.

Geo. E. Marshall,

S. E. Cor. State & Washington Sts.

Third Floor.   CHICAGO. ILL.